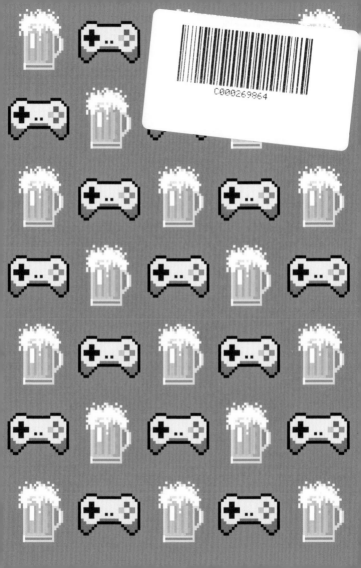

C000269864

A GAMER LOGS INTO A BAR...

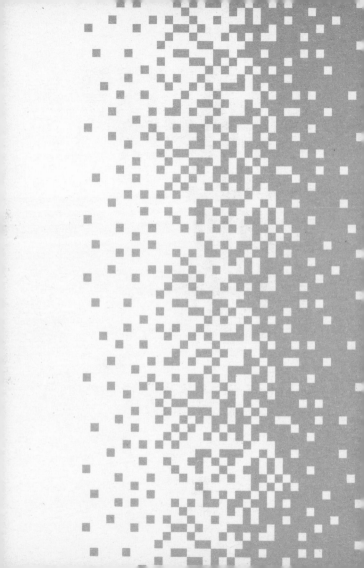

A GAMER LOGS INTO A BAR...

A JOKE BOOK

HarperCollins*Publishers*

HarperCollins*Publishers*
1 London Bridge Street
London SE1 9GF

www.harpercollins.co.uk

HarperCollins*Publishers*
1st Floor, Watermarque Building, Ringsend Road
Dublin 4, Ireland

First published by HarperCollins*Publishers* 2021

1 3 5 7 9 10 8 6 4 2

Jokes by Matt Growcoot © HarperCollins*Publishers* 2021
Illustrations by Ollie Mann © HarperCollins*Publishers* 2021

HarperCollins*Publishers* asserts the moral right
to be identified as the author of this work

A catalogue record of this book is
available from the British Library

ISBN 978-0-00-849113-0

Printed and bound in the UK using 100%
renewable electricity at CPI Group (UK) Ltd

MIX
Paper from
responsible sources
FSC™ C007454

This book is produced from independently certified FSC™ paper
to ensure responsible forest management.

For more information visit: www.harpercollins.co.uk/green

CONTENTS

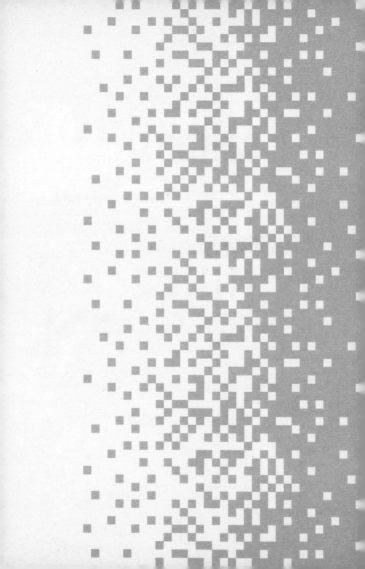

REAL-WORLD GAMER PROBLEMS

How do you respond when a bully tells you to 'get a life'?
I've got *plenty* of lives.

~~~~~~~~~~

What's the point in watching people play video games that you could play yourself?
Said the football fan.

~~~~~~~~~~

What do you call a gamer who doesn't let you play?
A control freak.

I just discovered my mum was having an affair.

You might think that was bad enough, but I found out in the WORST way. I was playing *Call of Duty* and another player told me he'd had intercourse with her. The worst part was he sounded so youthful.

What can be smelt and heard from ten miles away?

My husband playing *Call of Duty*.

Pre-pandemic, if you never left the house and played video games all day you'd be considered a loser.

In COVID times you're a hero.

Why couldn't the PC gamer stop weeping?
He refused to be consoled.

~~~~~~~~

Me: I'm going to be more adventurous and take risks.
Also me: *Waits at the red light on *Grand Theft Auto**

~~~~~~~~

What do you call gamers out together in public?
A rare occurrence.

People have always told me, 'Do something you love and you'll never work a day in your life!'

I play computer games all day and have never worked a day in my life.

What do you call it when a gamer gets into a fight?

An asthma attack.

My mum tells me she's so happy that I've stopped gaming for long enough to get out of my room and enjoy the outdoors.

She has absolutely no idea what *Pokémon Go* is.

What's a COVID denier's favourite video game?
Space Invaders.

~~~~~~~~~

Recently I've found I'm being haunted by Nintendo characters.
I should never have messed around with that Luigi board.

~~~~~~~~~

I laughed so hard at that last joke ...
... that now I have to console with my doctor.

My dad came to visit me at work last week, and I could have sworn he had a tear in his eye.

He told me, 'I can't get over you doing a real job now! It feels like only yesterday you were cooped up in your room, obsessed with those stupid computer games!'

I'm a VFX designer.

I'm not a player, I'm a gamer.
Players get the girls. I get bullied
at school.

~~~~~~~~~

**What do society and video-game
consoles have in common?**
No one can agree on which
generation is the best.

~~~~~~~~~

My daughter was really miserable.
I tried my best to cheer her up. I got her a
PlayStation, an Xbox – even a Nintendo
Switch. But she was inconsolable.

My husband said to me last night, 'I think I'm having a mid-life crisis. I'm so bored by my job and our marriage is getting stale. I wish life was more like a video game ...'

So I locked him in the bathroom and told him he'll have to pay £0.99 if he wants access to the rest of the house.

What do iPhone and *Call of Duty* fans have in common?
They both buy the same damn thing every year.

~~~~~~~~~~

My wife was playing a video game last night, and smashed up her keyboard when she was killed.
I'd say she definitely lost Control.

~~~~~~~~~~

I bought a broken Nintendo console ...
... so I had to get a Wiifund.

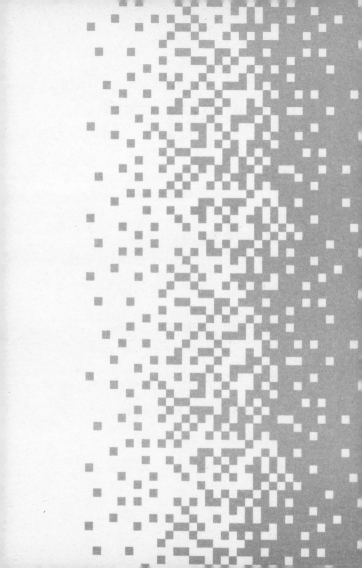

GAMER
RELATIONSHIPS

What's six blocks long and never gets laid?
The queue for the new *Call of Duty*.

~~~~~~~~~

My boyfriend dumped me because I bought the new Nintendo.
Ah well, it was time for a Switch.

~~~~~~~~~

My girlfriend left me because I always have video games on my mind.
Such an unnecessary thing to *Fallout 4*.

GAME OVER

My husband said he wanted a divorce, all because I spend every evening alone, gaming.

Looks like it was my *Destiny 2* be single.

What do you call a gamer struggling with erectile dysfunction?

A Try Hard.

My aunt keeps going on about how she's worried by all the violent games I play. Apparently she's read something about how they can lead to real-life murders.

My mum's not worried. She just replies, 'My son is constantly playing *The Sims: Hot Date*, and is no closer to getting a girlfriend!'

My gamer girlfriend just dumped me.
She said I always tried to controller.

~~~~~~~~~

What's the difference between the condom in a gamer's wallet and a conversation with an NPC?
Nothing, they're both totally pointless.

~~~~~~~~~

Why did my gamer boyfriend break up with me?
I didn't meet his Xboxtations.

I was chatting online with a girl and when I asked what her job was, she told me she was a model on Instagram.

I told her that I was a soldier in *Call of Duty*.

What's the difference between talking to an NPC and having sex with a gamer?

Nothing, they both leave you feeling awkward and disappointed.

A solicitor, an artist and a gamer are discussing whether it's worth having an affair. The solicitor is too worried about the possible repercussions if he's found out: expensive divorce proceedings and custody battles. The artist wants to find new passion and inspiration for his work, so is keen to give it a try. ›››

GAME OVER

The gamer tells them,
'Ah, I've got it good, lads!
My wife thinks I'm with
my mistress, my mistress
thinks I'm with my wife.
Meanwhile I can spend the
whole night gaming!'

My last relationship was like a computer game.
It started off real easy, but when it got harder I ended up cheating.

~~~~~~~~~~

I broke up with my girlfriend when her *Minesweeper* addiction got too bad.
I just knew it was a big red flag.

~~~~~~~~~~

If you can't handle being single, why not try committing a crime on *Grand Theft Auto*?
That way you'll know you're still wanted.

Over a coffee, Sid told Sarah he just had to break up with her.

Sarah: But why?

Sid: Because you're always playing computer games. And I'm just done with it!

Sarah: But – can I still see you in a *Fortnite*?

›››

Sid: No, I'm done with this.

Sarah: Well, this is a *Far Cry* from how I thought tonight was going to go. Can I still *Overwatch* you?

Sid: Why on earth would I let you do that? That's so creepy.

Sarah: Because it's my *Call of Duty*.

**The queues were massive for
the new *GTA V*.**
Gamers heard you could have sex in it,
and none of them wanted to die a virgin.

~~~~~~~~~~

Mario is red, Sonic is blue.
Press start to join and be my
player 2.

~~~~~~~~~~

**Did you hear about the bloke who
died playing an erotic video game?**
I guess you could say it was his
Final Fantasy.

Sometimes I wonder what our parents used to do for fun, back before video games were invented?

I asked my 16 siblings, but they weren't sure either.

Partner: Oh baby, I've had the most awful day.

Gamer: Oh no, babe, what happened?

Partner: How long have you got?

Gamer: About 20 minutes before my new game installs.

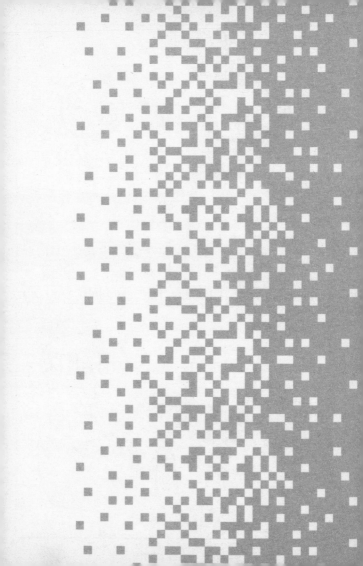

TOP
CHARACTERS

**What did Sonic use to knock
on the door?**
Knuckles.

~~~~~~~~~~

How do you get Pikachu on a bus?
You poke-em-on!

~~~~~~~~~~

**Why did Lara Croft start
looking up new jobs in
Archaeologists Weekly?**
Because her career was in ruins.

Who's faster, Sonic the Hedgehog or a cheetah?

A cheetah, of course. Sonic doesn't actually exist.

What was Mario's excuse when he dumped Princess Peach?

It's not you, it's-a-me, Mario!

~~~~~~~~~~

What is Master Chief's favourite band?

Slayer.

~~~~~~~~~~

What name did Wario give to his art supply shop?

World of Wario Crafts!

What noise does Solid Snake make when he laughs?

Ha-Hi-Hu-He-Ho.

Why did Princess Peach dump Mario for Toad?
He wasn't as much of a fun guy.

~~~~~~~~~~

What did Steve say to the Zombie?
Do you want a PIECE of me?

~~~~~~~~~~

What does Zelda always choose from the breakfast buffet?
A sausage Link!

Why did Frogger cross the road?

Because after an hour and a half you've finally completed the level.

How do the Mario Bros surf the internet?

Using a web Bowser.

~~~~~~~~~

Why would a grown-up want to play *Pokémon Go*?

Wynaut?

~~~~~~~~~

What happened when Mario parked his kart illegally?

It got Toad.

Why did Mario, Yoshi and Luigi meet up for the first time in fifteen years?

For a Wiiunion!

How do Koopas communicate?
Using a shell-phone.

~~~~~~~~

**What is Link's favourite
basketball play?**
His Hookshot!

~~~~~~~~

**What did Zelda tell Link to do when
he couldn't open the door?**
Triforce.

Did you hear, Sonic the Hedgehog and Curious George are going to be starring in a new Hollywood film together?

They're calling it
2 Fast 2 Curious.

What's Steve's favourite morning exercise routine?
He runs around the block.

~~~~~~~~~~

What's Mario's favourite musical?
Mamma Mia!

~~~~~~~~~~

What does Lara serve at dinner parties?
Croft Macaroni and Cheese.

What are Mario's favourite Simon & Garfunkel lyrics?

'Hello dark NES, my old friend.'

What did the green mushroom say to Luigi?
Get a life!

~~~~~~~~~~

Why did Dante refuse to chop up onions?
He thought the *Devil May Cry*.

~~~~~~~~~~

A creeper walks into a bar ...
Everybody dies.

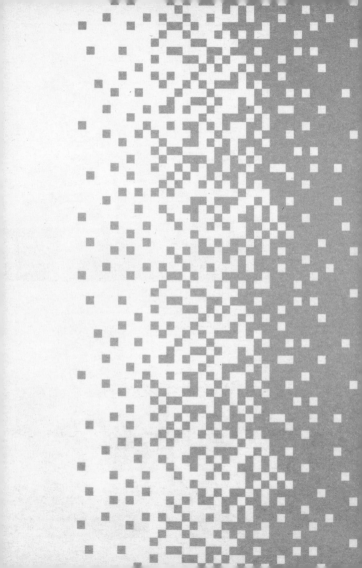

# #
GAMERLIFE

I think video games are so popular because you can let loose and indulge your wildest fantasies.

For example, on *The Sims*, you can have a job and a house.

I'm so bad at gaming ...
When I play *Grand Theft Auto*, I get
arrested for jaywalking.

~~~~~~~~

**How do you know someone is a
PC gamer?**
You don't, they tell you.

~~~~~~~~

**I've got a joke to tell you about
gaming ...**
But I'm waiting for the 32GB update
to install first ...

Why did the gamer pee their pants?

Because they couldn't pause their game.

Video games don't turn me into a violent person.

Lag does.

Sometimes I wonder if video games are a bad influence on the young.

But I grew up playing *Pac-Man* in the 80s, and it's not like my generation just went around in the dark listening to strange, repetitive music and munching pills ...

When is the best time of day to play Nintendo?
The Wii hours of the morning.

~~~~~~~~~~

What are the three Rs for a gamer?
Retry, Restart and Respawn.

~~~~~~~~~~

I don't need to 'get a life'.
I'm a gamer. I have plenty.

PAUSE

Mum: Sammy, Sammy, come quick, I need your help!

Gamer: I can't, Mum, I'm playing online.

Mum: But Sammy, I could die, I really need your help!

Gamer: If I pause my game, I will die!

What does a gamer eat with chips?
CoD.

~~~~~~~~~

If another person suggests video games make kids violent, I'll SMASH THEIR FACE IN!!
Wait ...

~~~~~~~~~

Sometimes I like to take my Nintendo Switch to the loo with me, so I can escape my kids for a few precious minutes.
Every parent needs a bit of Mii time.

I've got a great idea for an app: every few minutes it closes down whatever game you're playing and opens up a random new one.

It's going to be a gamechanger.

Video games have given me a real issue with authority.

The other day a woman introduced herself as my new 'Boss': I of course freaked out, drank a potion, then attacked her!

I asked my French friend if she liked video games.
'*Oui*,' she said. Which was unfortunate as I only have a Switch.

~~~~~~~~~

A gamer never dies!
They simply respawn.

~~~~~~~~~

I really hate it when ...
... autocorrect makes me say things I didn't Nintendo.

Call of Duty is such an environmentally friendly video-game franchise.

Every game is made from 90-per-cent recycled material.

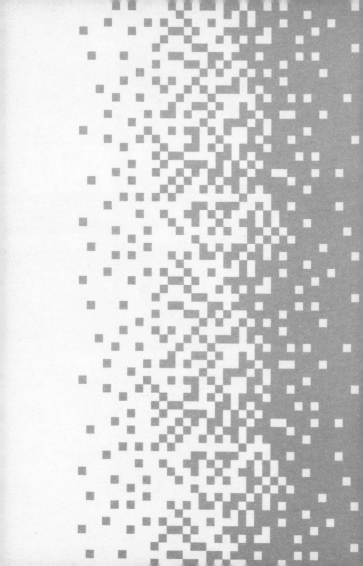

GEEKY GAMER JOKES

What did the Super Nintendo say to the Sega Genesis?

'I've always felt that I'm a bit better than you.'

What was the console gamer's New Year's resolution?
1280×720.

~~~~~~~~

A computer-game character walks into a bar ...
I should really turn noclip off.

~~~~~~~~

Gamers always get so annoyed when the game says, 'You can't go any further.'
I mean – come on! It's not the end of the world.

My friend told me that when you're playing video games, it's better to lose your health during spring, summer or winter.

I guess it makes sense. That way you don't have to worry about fall damage.

**What game do you play after
eating Brussels sprouts?**
Fartnite.

~~~~~~~~~~

**My brother always runs
sideways when he's playing
Call of Duty ...**
He's really D-pressing!

~~~~~~~~~~

Why can't PC gamers use Uber?
There are too many incompatible drivers.

My mum said she'd delete my computer games if I didn't iron my school clothes before dinner. I started off pretty well ...

But now I'm losing Steam.

What is a video-game art designer's favourite fizzy drink?
Sprite.

~~~~~~~~~

What did the gamer say when she took the COVID-19 vaccine?
NS.

~~~~~~~~~

I was going to make a Nintendo joke ...
But it was a Wii bit too hard for Mii to come up with one.

What's a Minesweeper?

It's either a computer game or an angry German janitor yelling at kids who nicked his broom.

Death Stranding is not a video game ...
It's a Hideo game.

~~~~~~~~~

There are ten kinds of gamers in the world.
Those that understand binary and those that don't.

~~~~~~~~~

What does a gamer say when they alt-tab by mistake?
wwwwwwwwwwwwwwwwww.

What do you call it when shops start replenishing their shelves with the Nintendo Wii?

A Wiistock.

What noise does the Nintendo ambulance make?
WIIU WIIU WIIU WIIU.

~~~~~~~~~~

What do you call a *Minecraft* celebration?
A block party.

~~~~~~~~~~

What do you call an obstinate console?
A Nintendon't!

NAPOLEON
COMMANDED 43 BATTLES IN HIS LIFE

JULIUS CAESAR
COMMANDED 15 BATTLES IN HIS LIFE

ALEXANDER the GREAT
COMMANDED 9 BATTLES IN HIS LIFE

CARL
COMMANDED HUNDREDS OF ARMIES IN 14,623 BATTLE SIMULATIONS

What's the difference between a cow and *GTA V*?

You can't milk a cow for seven years.

How do you deal with hunger in *Minecraft*?

Three square meals.

~~~~~~~~

Nintendo used to make the Wii.

So I decided to make the Switch.

~~~~~~~~

What do you call a *Call of Duty* player's instant success of a rap single?

A Flashbanger.

What did the Nintendo Wii do when they stopped working?

They Wiitired ...

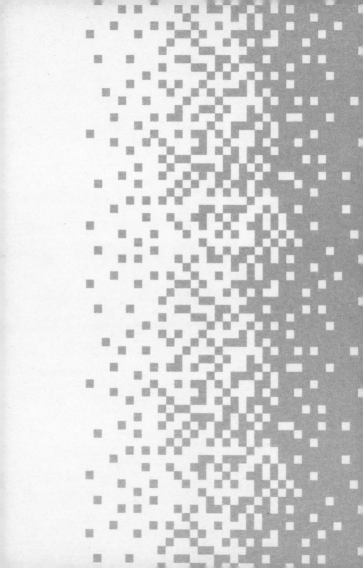

POP
CULTURE

What's Thanos's favourite first-person shooter game?
Half-Life.

~~~~~~~~~

What is Owen Wilson's favourite video game?
WoW.

~~~~~~~~~

Did you hear that *Minecraft* are making a movie?
I bet it's going to be a blockbuster.

What did Chewbacca win when he came top of the class in his first year training for the resistance?

Wookiee of the year.

I've got a great idea for a game where you can travel back to biblical times and kill Adam and Eve.

It's going to be the first ever first-person shooter.

Why are cats so great at video games?
Because they have nine lives!

~~~~~~~~~~

What did the Nintendo-loving mosquito say when he gave me a bite?
It's-a-me, Malario!

~~~~~~~~~~

What's the Nintendo Wii called in France?
A Nintendo yes!

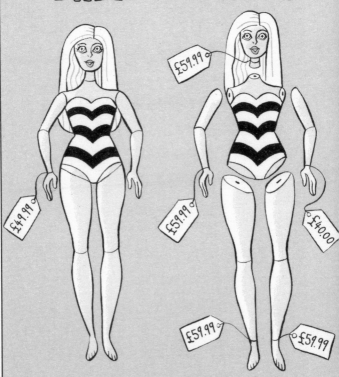

A gamer dies and goes to hell ...

After a single day the Devil has had enough; he calls God and says, 'Who is this lunatic you've sent down here? He's running around screaming, pushing walls, trying to kill demons and fight me, and keeps shouting, "Where the hell's the exit to level 2?"'

What does a communist say after rage-quitting a video game?
Not sure, but they'll probably be uninStalin the game.

~~~~~~~~~~

Why should you not bother trying to borrow money from Yoda?
He's always a little short.

~~~~~~~~~~

What do you say when you lose a Nintendo game?
I want a Wiimatch!

Jay-Z walks into a game store, goes up to the girl behind the counter and says, 'I need a Nintendo Switch. I can't find one anywhere!'

The girl leans forward and says, 'Listen ... if you're having game problems, I feel bad for you, son. I've got 90 Nintendos, but a Switch ain't one.'

Why are pirates not really into virtual reality?
They prefer AR.

~~~~~~~~~

What's the biggest arcade game in Mexico?
Guac-a-Mole.

~~~~~~~~~

Why is a Jedi knight never lonely?
The Force is always with him.

My dad thinks I play video games too much. The other night he told me, 'What are you really achieving, playing the same games night after night? When Mozart was your age he'd already written his first symphony!'

I replied, 'Yeah, well, by the time he was your age, he'd written 41 of them.'

A doctor once asked Quasimodo if he thought playing video games might have damaged his health. Quasimodo said he was pretty sure they had.

But when the doctor asked why he thought that, Quasimodo replied, 'Oh, I've just got a hunch.'

ADULT-GAMER-ONLY JOKES

WARNING:

THESE ARE PRETTY RUDE

Sex is like a video game for me.
I tend to just watch gameplay footage,
and never have a go myself.

~~~~~~~

**I think video games like *Call of
Duty* set an awful example for
children.**
When you shoot someone in real life,
there's no lag.

~~~~~~~

**What's white and smells like
Peach?**
Mario's Glove.

I've crashed my car multiple times, had sex with four prostitutes and I've been arrested ... I think that's enough practice ...

When I'm released I'm going to go home to play *GTA V.*

What would have been Adolf Hitler's favourite video game?
Mein Kraft.

~~~~~~~~~~

Why can't PC gamers have sex?
Because they're Microsoft.

~~~~~~~~~~

In a recent survey, three thousand teenage gamers were asked what they had done the previous day.
Ninety-six per cent said,
'Your mum'.

I got so pissed off playing *Call of Duty* that I spent quite some time telling my opponent (in detail) about how I was going to f*ck the brains out of his mum!

My son won't stop crying now.

What do video games and penises have in common?

The more you play with them, the harder they get.

~~~~~~~~~

What caused Princess Peach to choke?

Mario coming down the wrong pipe.

~~~~~~~~~

After his divorce, what did the gamer call his wife's vagina?

His Xbox.

Sex should be like Nintendo 64 classic ...

Great fun, and every issue solved by blowing and shoving it back in.

Gamers everywhere celebrated when Nintendo 64 celebrated its eighteenth birthday ...

As it meant they could now legally blow the cartridges.

~~~~~~~~

Rockstar have announced a GTA spinoff about breaking and entering.

They've called it *GTFO*.

~~~~~~~~

What do nymphomaniacs and Nintendo fans have in common?

They both lose their shit when they hear the word 'smash'.

Did you ever hear about the guy who got turned on by faulty buttons on controllers?

They say he got off to a bad start.

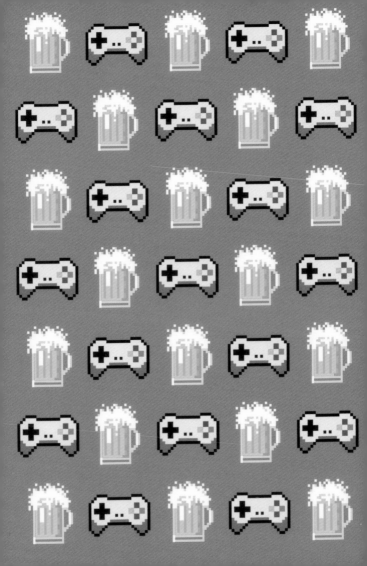